"If you're serious about calming down and creating your own personal oasis, you don't want to miss the *28 Day Guide*. Filled with simple ideas and lots of inspiration, it's the perfect companion to *OASIS in the Overwhelm* and is sure to keep you on track."

Wendy Battles, Optimal Health Coach
Healthy Endeavors

"Inside this little book is a big gift. Choose now to read and heed it, and you will give an enduring treasure to the person you will one day become. Millie Grenough's four gentle, scientific, and simple exercises will give strength and shape to the future you, who will look back and thank today's you for wising up and finding simple paths to healthy body and soul."

Sidney MacDonald Baker, MD
Author, *Detoxification & Healing* and *The Circadian Prescription*

"*OASIS in the Overwhelm 28 Day Guide* is a daily gentle reminder to exercise self-care and to develop new habits to better manage stress and create space in your life for the things that matter most."

Karen Senteio, Personal and Business Coach
President, VERVE, LLC

"Millie has done an outstanding job illuminating the reality of the pressures of today and has provided a great recipe and guide in aiding us all on how to develop that personal oasis we all know we need. Written in an easy and relaxing style, this is a must read, 'put it into action' book! Thank you for helping me find my oasis. I needed that!"

Barry Foster, Director
The Corporate Coaching Center

The *"OASIS 28 Day Guide* serves as the healing touch and genuine reminder of the truth that centers me daily in my hectic and often overwhelming life. It is a practical guide with real life-giving answers to cope and respond to our ever-changing existence."

Jane Petrozzi
Single Mom of a School-age Child and
Full-Time Project Manager

"For us recovering workaholics, Millie provides an invaluable service by coaching us to become more effective in the workplace while also helping us to fit work into a more appropriate place in the framework of our lives."

David Nee, Executive Director
William Caspar Graustein Memorial Fund

"Invest a couple of hours to change your life forever. We all know that stress kills so give a copy of *OASIS* to someone you love."

BJ Frazier, President
Just for the Health of It

"Any new book about stress and how to cope with it in our increasingly complex world must be welcomed with open arms. *OASIS* suggests simple steps that anyone of any age or walk of life can master. It works."

Elayne Phillips, Theatre Director
Bern, Switzerland

"One of the reasons I think many people will love *OASIS* is that it simply organizes various thoughts, methods and practices that people like me have been using in a desultory fashion to try to keep sane."

Anne Tyler Calabresi, Community Volunteer

"I use the 3-B-C strategy regularly now and have noticed a definite and immediate improvement as I move through my hectic days managing my staff."

Ginger Mierzejewski, Manager
American Payment Systems

"Imagine a group of executives sitting around a conference table, quietly taking deep breaths while gazing at a stone! I smiled as I witnessed, firsthand, the transformation of stressed and chaotic energy into a state of relaxation, calmness, and focus in sixty seconds. They embraced one strategy that Millie offers in her brilliant and useful book, *OASIS in the Overwhelm*."

Carole Jacoby, Master Certified Coach
President of Life Visions

"There is practical and simple information available in this book to help restore you on your journey through life."

Bernie Siegel, MD, Author
Love, Medicine & Miracles and *365 Prescriptions for the Soul*

"The *OASIS 28 Day Guide* is simple, in the sense of being a really doable process to commit to, and rich at the same time. I love the powerful questions you ask and the inspirational quotes and affirmations. I especially like the piece in the **tune in often** section where you suggest choosing a strategy for different stress scenarios. I'm going to copy and post that as a reminder for myself."

Jackie Rubell Johnson, CPCC
Choice Business and Personal Coaching, LLC

"Stressed? Swamped with to-do lists? Too many problems you feel you don't have control over? Millie Grenough's *OASIS in the Overwhelm* will give you just the breath of fresh air you need to get you back on your feet – and feel better."

Dennis Schleicher, Author
Support Group Counselor

"The OASIS Strategies are easy, effective, and bring results. The *28 Day Guide* keeps you on track to achieve more calm and less chaos in just one month!"

Monica Tari, Therapist and Life Coach

"Millie Grenough offers a welcome oasis to our crazy pace. Grenough brings her vast academic and personal experience full circle to offer four simple skills that can be applied anywhere by anybody."

Jane Larson de Torres
Language Consultant, Barcelona, Spain

"My most significant teaching that I take away is the concept that stress is a natural part of life. I have been working on reframing the way that I look at the stresses I face daily. I realize now that it is a blessing to be faced with the stresses in my life. My challenge is managing these stresses rather than regretting them. Thank you for opening my eyes to a different way of seeing."

Sonjia Smith, Community Activist
Mother of Four Children

"A great read if your life is crazy and you want to relax. I have already practiced each of the book's four techniques and my wife has noticed the difference. I am recommending *OASIS* to my Mother and Mother-in-law who both recently lost their husbands and are in search of the Oasis in the Overwhelm of their daily lives. I hope they get as much out of it as I did."

John Cirello, Senior Partner
Cirello & Vessicchio, LLC, and Father of Two Young Children

What a whiff of fresh air . . . *OASIS* comes as 'a clear stream of reason' in 'the dreary desert sand of dead habit.'"

D. Murali, Financial Daily Reviewer
The Hindu Business Line

Profound and effective! These strategies are the perfect cure for our crazy-busy lives."

Mike Song, Co-author
The Hamster Revolution:
How to Manage Your Email Before It Manages You

"Looking for bits of balance in the daily chaos? Millie's OASIS Strategies give you short, sixty-second breaks from the zaniness of life – and, as a bonus, they're practical ideas to be happier."

Jim Donovan, *Handbook to a Happier Life:*
A Simple Guide to Creating the Life You've Always Wanted

oasis

IN THE OVERWHELM

28 Day Guide

*Rewire Your Brain
from Chaos to Calm*

Beaver Hill Press

oasis

IN THE OVERWHELM

28 Day Guide

*Rewire Your Brain
from Chaos to Calm*

MILLIE GRENOUGH

with

JILL BERQUIST & VIRGINIA KRAVITZ

Beaver Hill Press

OASIS in the Overwhelm
28 Day Guide: Rewire Your Brain from Chaos to Calm

Published by Beaver Hill Press
orders@oasisintheoverwhelm.com
www.oasisintheoverwhelm.com

Printed and bound in the USA on acid-free paper by King Printing
Cover watercolor by Randi Parker
Cover design by Elements LLC, Peggy Bloomer and Renee O'Connell
Interior design by Dorothy Scott

The information contained in this book is intended for informational purposes only. If you have questions regarding a medical condition, please consult your health professional.

Library of Congress Cataloging-in-Publication Data
Grenough, Millie   Berquist, Jill   Kravitz, Virginia
OASIS in the Overwhelm 28 Day Guide: Rewire Your Brain from Chaos to Calm
ISBN 978-0-9778411-1-0

1. Body/Mind.   2. Life Coaching.   3. Stress Management.
I. Grenough, Millie.   II. Berquist, Jill.   III. Kravitz, Virginia.   IV. Title.

"You can't stop the waves
but you can learn to surf."

Jon Kabat-Zinn, Ph.D.

We thank our colleagues who added their wisdom and practical ideas to this Guide: Wendy Battles, Tom Campbell, Bob Erdmann, Jackie Johnson, Lynda Ashby Ludy, Terry Nolan, Renee O'Connell, Jane Petrozzi, Laurie Reiss, and Karen Senteio.

contents

This Guide is intended to be used in tandem with the book *OASIS in the Overwhelm.* For added support, the audio CD of *OASIS* guides you through the strategies and provides tips for making them part of your daily life.

note from millie

YOU'RE TOO BUSY? Don't have time to do anything else?

I'm in the same boat. And there are millions of other folks like us. That's why I "created" the OASIS 60-second Strategies.

Well, actually it first took a near-death accident to make me slow down. During my recuperation time, I finally got it that unless I did something different, I might not be around much longer. The something different turned into the OASIS Strategies. I have had success with them, and now I want to share them with you.

The OASIS Strategies are a kind of Jumpstart Sanity Kit for us fast-movers:

- They honestly do take only 60 seconds each.

- They're easy to learn.

- They're a fast track to *re-wiring our brains* from chaos to calm.

The latest research in neuroscience lets us know that, no matter how old we are, *we have the power to re-wire our own brains.* Brain images verify the astounding fact that our brains are "plastic." By what we do, and even by what we think, we have the power to shape how they operate.

The OASIS Strategies will give you personal experience of your own brain's neuroplasticity. Every time that you do an OASIS Strategy, you are actually re-wiring your brain towards health. In the short space of 28 days, you can replace old "stuck" habits with enjoyable, powerful new grooves.

My book and CD *OASIS in the Overwhelm* have already helped hundreds of people add balance and enjoyment to their daily lives. Brad, the VP of an engineering firm and father of two teen-agers says,

> "OASIS is an excellent guide for Type A people like me who want quick and practical methods to manage stress. They really work!"

Mimi, a realtor, freelance writer and mother of three young children, adds,

> "Let me just say that I LOVE the title. As soon as I read that, I felt more at peace. The word alone is something of a mantra, immediately conjuring up feelings of peace and sanctuary. I LOVE it."

YOU MIGHT ASK, if the OASIS Strategies are so simple, and the book and CD are out there, why this Guide?

Answer: Because practicing the Strategies on a daily basis will help you make them an easy and effective part of your life. It will help you create the intention, the time, and the space to really integrate these strategies into your days. And, as you do, you will feel the difference as you re-wire your own brain towards fuller health and greater happiness.

I ASKED MY GOOD FRIENDS AND LIFE COACH COLLEAGUES, Jill Berquist and Virginia Kravitz, to help create this OASIS Guide. Jill and Ginny are veteran travelers on the OASIS journey. They were in the Pioneer Group of my ongoing training program *OASIS: Training the Trainers*; they continue to make OASIS a vibrant part of their daily lives. As Authorized OASIS Trainers, they now help individuals and groups find their own oases.

Millie

A little P.S. It took a near-fatal accident for me to wise up and change my way of living. I am happy that you are not as hard-headed as I was. Wherever you are in your life, you are choosing right now to take more loving – and wiser – care of yourself. Now that's using your brain.

Congratulations!

Welcome to your own OASIS.

> Every instant of your life you face multiple choices. At each decision point, you either remain in a familiar pattern or you opt for a new route.
>
> Millie Grenough, Author
> *OASIS in the Overwhelm*

introduction

BEFORE YOU BEGIN PRACTICING the OASIS Strategies, here is an overview of what you can expect over the next 28 days.

The first steps (pages 21-32) are an opportunity to examine the role that overwhelm plays in your life and sharpen your motivation for creating new responses.

The following 28 days (pages 33-102) provide you with an easy format for integrating the OASIS Strategies. Here you'll find directions for each strategy along with affirmations that gently remind you to create your OASIS even in challenging circumstances. There are also examples of how to make the strategies work for you in everyday situations, as well as a place to capture your thoughts as you go along. Recording your personal experience with the strategies will help reinforce the new habits you are developing.

Living your OASIS (pages 103-107) offers ideas for continuing to build the OASIS Strategies into your everyday life.

> Sure, we all live 24/7 lives. No doubt about it. The real question is "What do you want those twenty-four hours and seven days to be?"
>
> Jane Baron Rechtmann
> Wife, Mother of Two Sons, High School Teacher

TO GET THE MOST OUT OF THE GUIDE, we invite you to:

- Make the commitment to take yourself seriously.
- Be clear with your intention.
- Select the same time each day to use your OASIS Guide. You may find that first thing in the morning works best to start you off well on your day.

Know that:

- You indeed have the power to control your attitude and your actions, and the ability to establish healthier re-wiring as the pathway of preferred usage in your brain.

When you do that:

- You will experience increased calm, fuller health, and greater happiness.
- The people around you will be glad that you are doing it.
- You are adding your part to peace in our world.

The power of willful activity to shape the brain remains the working principle not only of early brain development, but also of brain function as an ongoing, living process.

Dr. Jeffrey Schwartz & Sharon Begley in *The Mind and the Brain: Neuroplasticity and the Power of Mental Force*

first steps

warm up

FIND A RESTFUL PLACE to sit down. Take a few deep breaths and allow yourself to settle in. Now that your mind and body are clearer, you're ready to focus your intention. Take time now to ask yourself:

Question #1:

At this precise moment in my life, what are my toughest challenges/problems/stressors?

Pinpoint your current personal realities. Include your health, your work, your family, your financial status, your thoughts about the future. Make your responses very specific, for example:

- *I don't have time to do all I need to do.*
- *I feel out of shape and haven't been able to stick with an exercise program.*
- *I'm very concerned about my _____ (daughter, son, spouse, friend, parent).*
- *My financial situation is stressing me out.*
- *I want to change careers but I don't know what else I could do.*

Write down your answers. Writing your problems down will help get them out of your head and into fresh air.

Do you know that stress in humans:

- contributes to 80% of major illnesses,
- is responsible for 75% to 90% of visits to doctors' offices, and
- costs businesses as much as $300 billion a year?

Smart Money Magazine

Question #2:

At this precise moment in my life, what are my chief "cosmic" worries?

Include everything that is outside your family and your work. Think about your neighborhood, your city, your country, the world. As you consider this larger universe, again be very specific. Jot down your responses.

A FRIENDLY WARNING: As you do this, your agitation may appear to increase. Remember: this clarification process isn't creating the problems; it simply names them. Unidentified stressors have a way of sucking up tremendous amounts of energy. Whether you are conscious of them or not, background rumblings have a significant impact on your balance and your health.

As you identify the sources of your discomfort, you gain increased control over the background static. You put yourself in the driver's seat.

Question #3:

WHAT DO YOU WANT **from reading this Guide?**

If you say,

- *I want to feel better,* or
- *I want to be more balanced,*

that won't cut it.

Get real, get definite. Make your intentions specific, even if they seem small. For example, I want to:

- *Develop a routine for beginning my workday with positive energy.*
- *Schedule three periods of "me time" during the week.*
- *Decide on two specific ways to spend time with my family.*
- *Find a calm way to deal with email.*
- *Shake my habit of taking problems to bed with me.*

Write down two or three specific goals. When you target your goals clearly, you greatly improve your chances of achieving them.

what is possible

WHEN YOU GET CLEAR ON *WHY* you want to learn something new, you automatically increase your commitment level as well as the likelihood of your success with the new approach. Please take a moment now to solidify your reasons for engaging in this work by answering the following questions.

1. What is drawing me now to learn the OASIS Strategies?

2. What will it mean to me to improve how I deal with stress and conflicting demands in my life? Specifically:

   • If I don't feel so overwhelmed all the time, how will I feel?

   • What will be possible that isn't possible now?

- What will my family, friends, and co-workers notice?

3. What specifically do I foresee over time if I don't learn a better way to handle my stress and overwhelm?

> Neuroscientists believed until very recently that we are born with a certain number of neurons, and that's all we have for the rest of our life. Over the last two years we have discovered that to be false. It has now been demonstrated in humans that new neurons do grow throughout the entire life span. This is a fantastic new finding.
>
> Dr. Richard Davidson, University of Wisconsin

acknowledge your strengths

WHAT STRENGTHS DO I CURRENTLY POSSESS that support me during stressful periods? For example:

- *I tend to be resilient and usually land on my feet.*
- *I'm very organized and I prioritize well.*
- *I have supportive people in my life and I'm not afraid to ask for help.*
-
-
-
-
-

WHAT ARE SOME EFFECTIVE COPING STRATEGIES or proactive techniques I use when I feel overwhelmed? For example:

- *I take a small break to clear my head and walk away from my desk.*
- *I take a deep breath.*
- *I call a friend to help me regain perspective.*
-
-
-
-
-

what areas would I like to improve?

WHAT ARE MY VULNERABLE POINTS? For example:

- *I have a hard time saying no.*

- *I often feel responsible for things that are outside my control.*

- *I tend to overcommit.*

-

-

-

-

If your blood pressure rises to 180/120 when you are springing away from a lion, you are being adaptive, but if it is 180/120 every time you see the mess in your teenager's bedroom, you could be heading for a cardiovascular disaster.

Dr. Robert M. Sapolsky
in *Why Zebras Don't Get Ulcers*

self-assessment

AS YOU PROCEED THROUGH THIS GUIDE, you'll notice that the OASIS Strategies integrate four domains: physical, intellectual, emotional, and spiritual. Please review these four areas as portrayed below and place a checkmark near the statements that you feel are true for you on the whole (true at least 80% of the time). You may also add your own observations.

PHYSICAL WELL-BEING

____   I exercise regularly (aerobic, stretching, strength).

____   I usually get enough sleep and wake up feeling rested.

____   I eat well and have a fairly balanced diet.

____   I address health issues when they arise.

____   I'm satisfied with my energy level.

EMOTIONAL WELL-BEING

____   I am confident in my ability to communicate effectively with others, even when under pressure.

____   I have learned from the past and have resolved or let go of old issues.

____   I can see the humor in life and I often enjoy a good laugh.

____   When I feel unpleasant emotions (such as anger, sadness, frustration) I am able to step back, gain perspective, and determine what I need.

____   I have friends, family, and/or colleagues whom I call upon for support.

INTELLECTUAL WELL-BEING

_____ I am as organized as I want to be and easily keep track of appointments and projects.

_____ I rarely second guess decisions I make.

_____ I can count on my brain working clearly when I need to focus.

_____ When faced with problems, I am able to form a strategy for solving them.

_____ I seek out new things to learn and enjoy.

SPIRITUAL WELL-BEING

_____ I am aware of the activities that nourish my spirit and help me feel peaceful or connected.

_____ I engage in these activities often enough to have a positive impact in my life.

_____ I claim some quiet time every day (at least 5-20 minutes). I use this time to be silent, reflect, pray, meditate, or just "be".

_____ I get outside regularly to breathe fresh air and appreciate my natural surroundings.

_____ I am conscious of feeling grateful for many things in my life.

All people have a natural capacity for self-healing and self-regulation. The ultimate responsibility for change rests with each individual person.

Ilana Rubenfeld, Founder of Rubenfeld Synergy Method®

assessment reflection

- Acknowledge the domains in which you are already doing well. Keep them going.

- Notice a domain you need to build up. Make a specific plan to get it going.

- As you practice the OASIS Strategies, use them to support you in strengthening these specific areas.

Congratulations on taking the time to reflect, assess, and prepare.

You are now ready to move forward on your OASIS journey.

The brain allocates neural real estate depending on what we use most. In terms of which neural circuits endure and enlarge, you can call it survival of the busiest.

Sharon Begley
The Wall Street Journal, October 11, 2002

Notes & Insights:

4-D

4-D STANDS FOR "FOUR DIRECTIONS." Quite simply, 4-D invites you to shake off staleness in your body and mind and to stretch yourself into a much larger universe.

Use 4-D when you wish to:

- Stretch your body.

- Give your body a break.

- "Rinse off" your mind.

- Relax tense muscles.

- Clear mental clutter.

- Shake up your thinking.

- Gain a larger view.

- Spark creativity.

- Reset your emotions.

Research shows that usually we remember only:
    10% of what we read,
    26% of what we hear,
    30% of what we see, and
    50% of what we see and hear.

On the other hand, we remember 90% of what we say while doing a related activity.

                                        Edgar Dale in *Cone of Learning*

Here's how you do it:

full-body 4-D

PREPARE: STAND, INHALE AND EXHALE DEEPLY, letting worries sail out with each exhale.

Take a few more preparatory breaths, inhaling through the nose, and exhaling through loose lips. Pay attention to your body. Let arms dangle loosely, make space for your spine, neck and head to lengthen, and imagine space between each vertebrae. Let your weight go to gravity. Now that you are firmly planted, continue with the 4-D:

1. Stretch your arms and entire body to the ceiling, to the sky, as you say the word, **"North!"** out loud in a full voice. Feel the stretch. Exhale, letting your tension and worries release . . .

2. Bend at the waist, letting your head and torso drop towards the floor as you say, **"South!"** Go down as far as your body allows. Let your head feel heavy and hang. Exhale and come back to standing with an inhale . . .

3. Stretch out both arms in front of you, extending your fingers as far as they can reach. Then swing your torso to the east, saying, **"East!"** Notice how far out to the horizon you can see; ignore any clutter in your view. Come back to center with your arms in front of you . . .

4. Now swing your arms, and your whole upper torso to the west, and say, **"West!"** Really reach out to the West Coast and beyond the coast to the ocean and sky.

   Stretch with your arms, your torso and clear down to your feet. Enjoy your body's ability to experience the world from different vantage points. Come back to center and feel your feet solidly on the ground. Take another breath or two to enjoy yourself . . .

making 4-D work for you

Look to the next few days and note the types of specific situations when you might be able to use the 4-D Strategy. What are the positive results you might gain?

Situation	**Results I Expect**
I'm in a rush to get to work	*I'll cool down a bit. My body will feel looser.*

_____

_____

_____

_____

_____

_____

_____

OASIS Tip: ENGAGE THE BUDDY SYSTEM. It is easy to let your day slip away from you without a strategy here and there, especially when you are busy. Have a friend or co-worker keep you on track.

Example: MARY AND PAULA ARE MOMS who manage multiple kids and their homes. In the flurry of their busy days between appointments, chauffeuring to sports events, volunteering or personal meetings, one will contact the other just to check-in. She'll mention that she is stopping for a 4-D stretch to get a quick recharge in her day, and ask, "Did you do your 4-Ds today?" This serves as an instant reminder to the receiver and a reinforcement to the caller.

How will *you* remember to do these when you need to? With even the best intentions, what barriers might get in the way? What support structure (people, reminders) will help you?

day 2   **date** _____

SOME TIME DURING YOUR FIRST HALF HOUR of waking today, why don't you jump right in and try doing a 4-D to stretch and clear your mind to start your day? See how it goes.

If you are inclined, you can do the reflection, journaling and affirmation here, right after your 4-D, and then roll into your day. After the day is done and you have woven in some other time to practice, you can journal some more if you like.

Keep your OASIS Guide with you, and you can just fill in the blanks as you go.

Beginning of Day Reflection:

When it comes to potential stressors, today I will approach my day with the attitude that I am excited to try some new things. I know that by doing the 4-D it is possible that:

_____

_____

_____

_____

_____

_____

_____

_____

FOR TODAY:

Time I will use a 4-D: *lunchtime*

How will I remember? *my alarm in Outlook*

Results I expect: *I will be clear, more alert*

Time: _____

Reminder: _____

Results I expect: _____

Affirmation:

I am open and fluid today.
I am looking forward to playing with the 4-D.

Notes & Insights:

day 3 date _____

Beginning of Day Reflection:

As I start my day, some of the things I have on my mind this morning are:

_____

_____

_____

_____

_____

_____

Today I will play with the 4-D Strategy again. I expect that the benefits for me today will be:

_____

_____

_____

_____

_____

_____

Affirmation:

I am shaking up my ways of thinking.

Notes & Insights:

What am I noticing as I play with the 4-D?

What is working well for me?

day 4   **date** _____

variations of the 4-D

SOMETIMES YOU ARE NOT IN A SITUATION WHERE YOU CAN STAND UP, stretch out completely, or even speak aloud. At these times, there are other ways you can use the 4-D Strategy. In a smaller space, in a meeting or at your desk, you can do it with your head bending each direction at your neck. You can also do a 4-D with just your hands and wrists, or even with your feet and ankles.

OASIS Tip: CUSTOMIZE THE STRATEGY. Use a version that suits your situation best.

Example 1: MARCIA IS A COPYWRITER and is at her computer during much of her days. She occasionally will do a full-body, traditional 4-D, but even more often, she fits in one that involves her head, neck and shoulders, looking up, down and rolling to the left and right. In between each direction she remembers to breathe deeply.

Example 2: AS A PROGRAM MANAGER for a medical products company, Steve is in meetings practically all day long. Since he can't do a traditional 4-D very often, during his meetings he will do a 4-D with his hands or feet under the table. Steve says it helps him clear his head or just circulate his system. He says it can keep him fresh and help him be a better contributor, especially during some of his longer meetings.

Beginning of Day Reflection:

I reach for all possibilities today. Some of the things I have to look forward to today are:

_____

_____

_____

_____

FOR TODAY:

Time I will use a 4-D: _____

_____

_____

How will I remember? _____

Results I expect: _____

_____

_____

_____

_____

_____

_____

Affirmation:

I look forward to the adventure the day holds for me.

Notes & Insights:

day 5   date _____

Beginning of Day Reflection:

AS I WELCOME MY DAY, I will do a 4-D and expect it to start
me off with an open, fluid and refreshed body and mind.
I expect opportunities to open up to me such as the
possibility of:

_____

_____

_____

_____

_____

_____

_____

_____

Affirmation

My body and mind are expansive to all that is new.

Mentally and physically I am limber and stretching myself
for my highest good.

Notes & Insights:

day 6

date _____

Beginning of Day Reflection:

I AWAKE TODAY feeling: _____

My body is feeling: _____

My mind is: _____

What I am most looking forward to today is: _____

_____

_____

_____

_____

_____

Affirmation:

As I move my body, I am recharged and renewed.

Notes & Insights:

day 7   **date** _____

Beginning of Day Reflection:

I WILL ENJOY CHOOSING WAYS to use 4-D in my life today, as I treat myself to this rinsing-off and expanding ritual. The last good feeling I had about this strategy was that it enabled me to: _____

_____

_____

_____

_____

_____

Affirmation:

Everything that stretches me today is a gift.

Notes & Insights:

The body, mind, emotions and spirit are part of a dynamically interrelated system. Essentially, every time a change is introduced at one level of a person's being, it has a ripple effect throughout the entire physical, emotional, mental and spiritual system, changing the equilibrium of the whole person.

Ilana Rubenfeld in *The Listening Hand: Self-Healing through the Rubenfeld Synergy Method of Talk and Touch*

3-B-C

3-B-C STANDS FOR "THREE-BREATH-COUNTDOWN." It's the instant remedy for feelings of panic, anxiety, anger, frustration, or intense sadness. Whenever you are caught in an intense emotion, 3-B-C can help you head off overwhelm.

The 3-B-C is perfect for when you:

- Are tense, agitated, or "locked up."
- Feel your muscles are tight.
- Notice your breathing is shallow.
- Need an immediate change in perspective.
- Want to press the reset button.

we'll begin with the Emergency 3-B-C

HERE'S HOW TO DO IT.

- Rest both hands on your belly . . . Bring your attention to your breath . . . Send it out . . . Let your lips be soft . . . Purse them open a tiny bit to let the air come out . . . Very gradually, let all the breath out . . . Your worries can exit with your exhale . . . Hear your breath going out . . . Let your hands feel your belly go in. This is the long exhale.

- Now you're ready for the inhale.

- Keep your hands on your belly . . . Close your lips gently. Let the air come in through your nostrils . . . softly . . . gently . . . no need to pull it in . . . Nature abhors a vacuum, so your belly will fill up on its own . . . Just allow room for the air to come in . . . easily . . . Let it come all the way down . . . Feel it pushing your hands out as your belly expands. That's the full inhale. You've got it. Just keep it going.

- Breathe out and in two more times, slowly, deliberately . . . Take time to reach easy emptiness on the exhale and spacious fullness on the inhale. Let the breath do its thing. It's been doing it for centuries. Your body is simply one of its latest vehicles.

OASIS Tip: BEGIN BY EXHALING FIRST in order to get rid of negative or extreme emotions that could throw you off balance. You are allowing your worries to exit along with the exhaled breath. This helps you to respond consciously rather than react impulsively.

Example: MONICA USES A 3-B-C whenever she's on the receiving end of "bad customer service." She gets really frustrated when she's on hold for a long time, only to be transferred to someone's voice mail again. As she's waiting to make contact with a human, she does a 3-B-C to put things in perspective.

Fear is excitement without breath.

Fritz Perls, Ph.D., Founder of Gestalt Therapy

making 3-B-C work for you

OASIS Tip: RANDY SAYS THAT PUTTING HIS HANDS ON HIS ABDOMEN helps him make the breath deeper, from the diaphragm, rather than taking a shallow breath. He says he can feel that a deeper breath cleanses his body more thoroughly.

Randy's favorite time to practice 3-B-C is in the morning at his computer, right after he reviews his schedule for the day. It helps him feel more in control and reminds him that he has choices.

When can you envision using the 3-B-C Strategy this week?

_____

_____

_____

_____

_____

_____

To practice the strategy right now, look ahead to a situation that you expect to be challenging for you. Picture it in as much detail as possible. Then see yourself doing a 3-B-C.

_____

_____

_____

_____

_____

_____

day 9   **date** _____

Beginning of Day Reflection:

MY INTENTION TODAY IS TO *CONSCIOUSLY RESPOND* rather than impulsively react. I will experiment with using the 3-B-C today as challenging situations arise.

FOR TODAY:

Time I will use the 3-B-C: *when I walk in the door at work*

How will I remember? *touching the door will be my signal to remember*

Results I expect: *a shift to calm*

Time: _____

Reminder: _____

Results I expect: _____

_____

_____

_____

_____

Example: RAYMOND OFTEN GETS VERY STRESSED right before making a difficult phone call or having an important conversation. He has now made it a habit to do a 3-B-C first and has noticed that taking a brief moment to collect himself helps him communicate more effectively with the other person.

Affirmation:

My breath is the gateway to a calmer perspective.

Notes & Insights:

day 10 date _____

As I complete my early morning 3-B-C, what do I notice?

What is one thing I am looking forward to today?

Example: JAMIE USED TO DREAD GOING TO BED because that was the time he was prone to anxiety, as he ran through all that needed to get done that week.

He started a new PM ritual of "tucking himself in" with a night time 3-B-C. As Jamie takes his three breaths, he calls to mind three good things from the day, such as situations he handled well or things for which he is grateful.

Jamie finds it much easier to drift to restful sleep this way and now, when he tucks his five-year-old son into bed, Jonathon asks his dad to stay while he does his own 3-B-C.

Affirmation:

As I gently let go of tension, I make room for peace.

Notes & Insights:

day 11   date _____

Beginning of Day Reflection:

I BEGIN MY DAY TODAY BY TAKING IN SOMETHING PLEASANT from my surroundings. As I look around the room, what appealing color or object catches my eye?

IN ADDITION TO EMERGENCY SITUATIONS, here are some other ways you can use a 3-B-C.

- **Preventive 3-B-C**
  This version also involves taking three deep breaths while placing your hands on your belly. However, in the preventive variation you **inhale first**, to bring in calmness. With the inhale, you take in an appealing image, such as a pleasant color or object that is near you. You are inviting its beauty to come into your breath and being.

- **Personal Palm Pilot**
  This version of the 3-B-C is essentially a **mini-vacation**. Think of a vacation place or favorite spot, rub your palms together, put them over your eyes, and "go" to that vacation spot for a moment, long enough to take a few deep breaths.

*Think of the above two variations of the
3-B-C as pleasurable workouts – something you can do
any time to strengthen your emotional muscles.*

PRACTICE A PREVENTIVE 3-B-C RIGHT NOW.

What am I noticing as I allow myself to take a few deep cleansing breaths?

What do I want to keep in mind as I approach my day today?

FOR TODAY:

Time I will use a 3-B-C: _____

How will I remember? _____

Results I expect: _____

_____

_____

_____

Affirmation:

Beauty increases when I take a moment to notice it.

Notes & Insights:

day 12   **date** _____

Beginning of Day Reflection:

TODAY I WILL REMEMBER that I can take a mini-vacation any time I choose.

Example: LESLIE, A SENIOR PRODUCTION MANAGER for a broadcast company, typically has a quick lunch at her desk. She recently began a new routine of taking a moment to do a mini-vacation 3-B-C right before she eats. She says this simple habit feels like a brief yet pleasant retreat and helps her feel refueled for the afternoon.

Affirmation:

I feed my soul by visiting beautiful places
in my imagination.

Notes & Insights:

day 13   date _____

Beginning of Day Reflection:

TODAY, EVEN WHEN I AM EXTREMELY BUSY and feel that I don't have time for absolutely anything, I will experiment with doing a **1-B-C** instead of a 3-B-C. I will use this brief pause to collect myself as I transition from one activity to another.

Example: TRACY IS A DEPARTMENT HEAD with a team of talented individuals who voice their opinions strongly and are prone to conflict. Tracy says the 1-B-C comes in handy for both of these situations.

When she is seeking to resolve conflict or disagrees with a colleague, she does a 1-B-C to respond openly and professionally rather than in a defensive manner.

When someone on her staff walks into her office and interrupts her focus, she quickly determines if it is an important conversation to have at that time. If so, she does a quick 1-B-C and says to herself, "I am present. I am listening." This helps her be fully attentive.

Affirmation:

Take a moment, take a breath.

Notes & Insights:

If you repeatedly turn on the stress response, or if you cannot appropriately turn off the stress response at the end of a stressful event, the stress response can eventually become nearly as damaging as the stressors themselves.

Dr. Robert M. Sapolsky
in *Why Zebras Don't Get Ulcers*

day 14   **date** _____

Beginning of Day Reflection:

TODAY I WILL NOTICE WHEN I SPONTANEOUSY AND NATURALLY gravitate to doing either a 3-B-C or a 1-B-C.

What am I learning from this simple practice?

What is within my control even when things are out of control?

Example: TONY IS A BUSY SALES EXECUTIVE who puts a lot of miles on his car and has a jam-packed schedule most days. He's found a way to make 3-B-C work for him throughout the day by abbreviating it to a 1-B-C.

As he moves from appointment to appointment and task to task, Tony takes a 1-B-C to transition. What he's noticed is that he is more present to each person he is meeting or to the project at hand. He says, "I'm moving consciously instead of just buzzing around. I feel more powerful and in control. I'm having more fun, too."

Affirmation:

My breath is my own internal metronome.
I can adjust my tempo whenever I need to.

Notes & Insights:

cue-2-do

THE CUE-2-DO STRATEGY INVITES YOU TO *USE* YOUR DISCOMFORT, your pains, your distress signals, to bring you to awareness and to move yourself towards pleasure.

Whenever you feel discomfort, whether it is physical or emotional, use the Cue-2-Do to:

- Really *get* how your emotions impact your body, and vice versa.

- Turn your *push-my-buttons reflexes* into life-saving signals.

- Shift yourself out of a stuck groove.

- Change channels from discomfort to pleasure.

- Gain greater control of your emotions.

prep work

TO USE THIS STRATEGY YOU WILL WANT TO BECOME FAMILIAR with *your* particular cues, *your* unique distress signals. You will want to know where they show up in your body and in your mind.

You will also want to be on friendlier terms with your palette of emotions and begin to understand how your signals and emotions dance with each other in your daily life.

The following two questions will help you get a better handle on this fascinating interplay.

1. What are *your* cues?

When you are in a difficult situation, where do you notice your discomfort, physically and mentally? Do you get tight shoulders? a headache? spacey mind? shallow breath? queasy stomach? clenched jaw?

When you are upset or angry, sad or confused, fearful or anxious, exactly *where* do you feel it?

Right now, take a few minutes to see if you can identify your distress signals. Precisely where do you notice them? Head? Stomach? Throat? Chest? Jaw? Neck or shoulders? Hands? Mind? Heart?

What specifically do you notice about each? Dull throbbing in your left temple? Cold sweat in your palms? We mean the *where* and *what* quite literally. Locate exactly where in your body or in your mind you become aware of discomfort. Find the words that best describe the feeling in that place. Write down your answers in as much detail as you can.

Now that you have pinpointed your cues, you're ready for the next step.

2. What are your *emotional channels* connected to these cues?

If you are like most people, you probably have a wide range of reactions to any particular situation. We call these reactions your *emotional channels*.

When you pay very close attention to yourself, you will probably notice that different situations set off different cues that trigger different emotional channels. The trick is to begin to notice your cues, and then try to determine what emotional channel they are lighting up.

> **Examples:** BRUCE SAYS, "WHEN I FEEL A POUNDING across the front of my forehead and a tightness in my fists, I can be pretty sure I'm angry at somebody."
>
> Neil knows: "When I suddenly notice that I've stopped breathing, I get it – I'm close to panic about something."
>
> When someone says something that feels hurtful to Amanda, she notices a variety of cues: "My stomach gets queasy, my throat tightens, and my mind starts to blur."

TO MAKE THIS REAL FOR YOU, go back to your list of cues that you wrote for Question 1. See if you can identify the emotional channel(s) usually connected to each. Write in the name of the channel(s) next to each cue.

Now that you have identified your personal cues and your emotional channels, you're ready to put into action the Cue-2-Do Strategy.

how to do the cue-2-do

TO MAKE THIS STRATEGY WORK FOR YOU, right now:

- Perform a thorough body/mind check. Notice if you are aware of any discomfort.

- If you detect an area of discomfort in your body or your mind, go with that.

- If not, think of a time in the recent past or a situation that may be looming in the future that you are upset or uncomfortable about. Go with that situation.

Now ask yourself the **5 Cue-to-Do Questions**:

1. What is *my cue* right now? Precisely *where* am I feeling it? Exactly what does it *feel like*?

   _____

   _____

   _____

   _____

2. What is that cue signaling? What *emotional channel* am I on? Anger? Worry? Frustration? Depression? Anxiety? Several emotional channels at once?

   _____

   _____

   _____

   _____

3. What's the *current drama* on that channel? Is it a rerun of a past event, a real-life situation right now that needs my immediate attention, or an uneasy fear of something that might happen if . . . ?

   _____

   _____

   _____

   _____

4. Is there anything *I can do* and *want to do right now* about this situation? If your answer is "Yes," then *take the appropriate action* immediately. If the answer is "No," then go to question 5. It may be time to *change channels.*

_____

_____

_____

_____

5. *What action* is best for me right now? Ask yourself: "What emotion do I want to let go of? What emotion do I want to invite in to replace it?" Then change channels immediately.

_____

_____

_____

_____

_____

making cue-2-do work for you

OASIS Tip: THIS WEEK, MEET YOUR BODY AND EMOTIONS in a fresh way. You might even imagine that you are going on a blind date with your body and your mind – no judgments, no pre-conceptions, just curiosity. Be open to whatever you may find. You may be surprised at your discoveries.

Example: TOM IS A GANGBUSTER GET-IT-DONE-NOW manager. When he pays attention to his cues, he now notices that a racing mind and agitated hands are often his signal that he's heading into impulsive reaction mode.

Instead of charging ahead or taking an aspirin, he now uses his mind-hands cue as a signal to stop. Then he asks himself the five Cue-2-Do questions.

Look ahead to your coming week. Note specific situations when it might be helpful to use the Cue-2-Do Strategy. What positive results might you gain?

_____

_____

_____

_____

_____

_____

_____

HOW WILL YOU REMEMBER to do the Cue-2-Do when you need to? Even with the best intentions, what barriers might get in the way? What support structure (people, reminders) will help you?

_____

_____

_____

_____

_____

_____

_____

The most powerful – and the most controllable – stressor in the world is the human mind.

M. Matteson & J. Ivacevich in *Controlling Work Stress*

day 16   **date** _____

Beginning of Day Reflection:

TODAY I WILL APPROACH MY CHALLENGES with the attitude that each challenge is an opportunity for me to know myself in a new way. I know that by paying attention to my physical cues, it is possible that:

_____

_____

_____

_____

_____

_____

FOR TODAY:

Time I will use Cue-2-Do: *when I get stuck in traffic*

How will I remember? *my stomach tightens*

Results I expect: *easier breathing, more patience*

Time: _____

Reminder: _____

Results I expect: _____

_____

_____

_____

Affirmation:

I am open and curious today.
I am looking forward to playing with Cue-2-Do.

Notes & Insights:

day 17   **date** _____

OASIS Tip: SOMETIMES WE'RE NOT TOTALLY AWARE of our bodily reactions and of how we express our emotions. Not to worry. If you have trouble identifying your particular signals and the emotional channels they're related to, try asking the people you live and work with. They can probably give you some clues!

Beginning of Day Reflection:

AS I BEGIN MY DAY, some of the things that I am noticing in my body right now are:

_____

_____

_____

_____

_____

_____

Today I will experiment with the Cue-2-Do Strategy again and I will pretend that I am on a blind date with my body. I expect that the benefits for me today will be:

_____

_____

_____

_____

_____

_____

_____

Affirmation:

I am noticing my body in a fresh new way.
I am receptive to my body's signals.

Notes & Insights:

day 18   date _____

Beginning of Day Reflection:

MY BODY IS BECOMING AN ALLY. I am enjoying my ability to converse with it. Some of the things I look forward to doing with my physical self today are, for example:

- *feeling the breeze on my skin*

- *noticing my heart beat*

_____

_____

_____

_____

_____

_____

_____

FOR TODAY:

Time I will use a Cue-2-Do: _____

How will I remember? _____

Results I expect: _____

_____

_____

_____

_____

_____

Affirmation:

I am beginning to know my body in a more complete way. I appreciate what it is telling me.

Example: WHENEVER SHE HEARD DISTURBING NEWS on the radio, Melissa used to slip into her depressed channel. She would often discover – after the fact – that her intestinal system took the brunt of her reaction.

Now she uses her churning stomach as a cue to ask: *Okay, what's going on right now? Is there anything I want to do and can do about it? If so, I'll do it.*

If not, I change from the depressed channel to a find-one-thing-that's okay channel.

It clears my head and my stomach immediately.

Notes & Insights:

Notes & Insights:

day 19   **date** _____

Beginning of Day Reflection:

AS I BEGIN MY DAY, I LOVINGLY PLACE MY HANDS on my body and I thank it for all that it does for me. I expect opportunities to open to me such as possibly:

_____

_____

_____

_____

_____

_____

Affirmation:

I am more confident in recognizing my body's cues.

Notes & Insights:

Notes & Insights:

day 20   **date** _____

Beginning of Day Reflection:

AS I BEGIN MY DAY, I LOOK AT MYSELF IN THE MIRROR and I tune in to the *gratitude channel*. I see myself with an open, fluid and refreshed body and mind. I expect opportunities to open to me today such as possibly:

_____

_____

_____

_____

_____

_____

_____

Example: ROAD RAGE WAS BRIAN'S LONGTIME COMPANION, so much so that even after he had several bad accidents, he felt more justified in having his anger.

Now, when a car shoots past him on the highway, Brian focuses on himself rather than on the other guy. The tightness in his eyes and his held breath remind Brian to use his Cue-2-Do instead of his knee-jerk hit-the-gas reflex.

Affirmation:

I marvel that I have the power to change my emotional channels.

Notes & Insights:

day 21   **date** _____

Beginning of Day Reflection:

AS I BEGIN MY DAY, I STAND WITH MY FEET FIRMLY AND
COMFORTABLY under me. I am in awe of the many wonders
inside me and outside me. I know that when I become
really present to whatever is happening now:

Affirmation:

My body and my mind are limber.
I am open to new possibilities.

Notes & Insights:

> By what we choose to do and not do, we influence which neurons grow and how much they grow.
>
> Dr. Jeffrey Schwartz
> UCLA School of Medicine

1 Stone

1 STONE IS THE SIMPLEST, and perhaps the most important of the *OASIS* Strategies. It's the ultimate *rinse cycle*. It can give you an immediate oasis, wherever you may be.

Use 1 Stone when you wish to:

- Unhinge yourself from the chaotic or hectic grip of the moment.
- Pull your attention from regretting the past or worrying about the future to the peace of the present.
- Have a touchstone to a healthy thought or feeling you want to remember.
- Use something tangible to cut through resistance or distraction.
- See the big picture.
- Alter your overall pace from fast to slower.
- Balance your total self.

You can observe a lot by watching.

Yogi Berra

here's how to do 1 Stone

- Place a stone or any object of comfort in the palm of your hand.

- With relaxed attention, look at the stone. Notice the variations in its color, its texture, its grain.

- Feel the stone in your hand. How heavy does it feel? Is it cool or warm?

- With your eyes open, breathe in and out very slowly as you look at the stone.

- Take nine more in-and-out breaths as you continue to look at the stone.

- If your mind wanders somewhere else, that's okay. That's what minds do. Just bring it back gently to the stone and your breath.

When you finish your ten breaths, stay with your stone a little bit longer.

What do you notice now about your body? Your breathing? Your heartbeat? Your thoughts?

Gradually let your eyes move to your surroundings. Keep on breathing as you let the larger picture come into your consciousness.

Take this easy awareness with you as you make the transition into the next moment of your day.

making 1 Stone work for you

OASIS Tip: CHOOSE AN OBJECT THAT HAS MEANING for you or has a texture you enjoy. Be creative.

Example: JAYNE HAS RIVER STONES ALL AROUND HER HOME in decorative bowls to have them handy whenever any one in her family wants to use one.

Her eight-year-old daughter Abby has her own collection of stones in a bag in her nightstand. Her daughter uses the stones when she is angry or frustrated and needs to calm herself.

Abby also loves to collect sea shells and she sometimes uses these for this exercise.

For this week, note the types of specific situations when you could use the 1 Stone Strategy.

What object or objects are you likely to use?

Where will you keep the object that you will be using and how will you remember to use it?

OASIS Tip: BE PATIENT WITH YOUR WANDERING MIND.

It is natural for your mind to wrestle with you when you want to keep it focused on any thought or object for more than a second or two.

Each time this happens, just gently notice it is wandering and ease it back to your object and your breath.

With practice, your mind will become better trained to stay with you longer and longer.

How will you remember to take the ten breaths and do 1 Stone when you need to?

day 23   **date** _____

Beginning of Day Reflection:

I LIVE IN A BIG WORLD WITH MANY THINGS GOING ON. Today I will gently call myself to the present in each moment.

FOR TODAY:

Time I will use the 1 Stone: *before doing my daily sales calls*

How will I remember? *leave stone on my call log*

Results I expect: *calm, better listening*

Time: _____

Reminder: _____

Results I expect: _____

_____

_____

_____

_____

_____

_____

_____

Affirmation:

All that was and all that will be is *now*.

Notes & Insights:

day 24   **date** _____

Beginning of Day Reflection:

AS I BEGIN MY DAY, some of the things I have on my mind this morning are:

_____

_____

_____

_____

_____

_____

_____

Today I will experiment with the 1 Stone Strategy again. I expect that the benefits for me today will be:

_____

_____

_____

_____

_____

_____

_____

Affirmation:

Every single moment holds an opportunity for
greater peace, awareness and clarity.

Notes & Insights:

day 25   **date** _____

Beginning of Day Reflection:

TODAY I WILL CONCENTRATE ON MY FOCUS AND PACE. Some of the benefits I will gain from slowing down and being mindful today are:

_____

_____

_____

_____

_____

_____

_____

_____

OASIS Tip: USE THE STRATEGY IN A WAY that integrates easily into your day. Make it personal.

Example: Mark is an IT Executive at a financial services company. He finds himself in a harried pace most of the time and moves from meeting to meeting on most days. He does 1 Stone at his desk between meetings to catch his breath and get back to the present moment.

Even when Mark is in a meeting he can touch the stone in his shirt pocket to remind him to focus, breathe deeply and slow his pace.

Breathing in, I calm my body.
Breathing out, I smile.

Thich Nhat Hanh

FOR TODAY:

Time I will use 1 Stone: _____

How will I remember? _____

Results I expect: _____

_____

_____

_____

_____

_____

_____

Affirmation:

My power is in the present.

Notes & Insights:

day 26   **date** _____

Beginning of Day Reflection:

AS I OPEN MY DAY, I will do 1 Stone and expect it to start me off with a grounded and peaceful lens for my day. I expect opportunities to open up to me today such as:

_____

_____

_____

_____

_____

_____

_____

_____

Affirmation:

Peace breathes through me effortlessly as I inhale.
Worry leaves me effortlessly as I exhale.

Notes & Insights:

day 27   **date** _____

Beginning of Day Reflection:

I AWOKE TODAY FEELING: _____

My body is feeling: _____

_____

_____

_____

_____

_____

My mind is: _____

_____

_____

_____

_____

What I am most looking forward to today is: _____

_____

_____

_____

_____

Affirmation:

When I gaze at my river stone, I see deeper into me.

Notes & Insights:

day 28   **date** _____

Beginning of Day Reflection:

I WILL ENJOY CHOOSING TIMES to use 1 Stone in my life today, as I look forward to this grounding and balancing ritual. I know that the benefits I gain from it are the following:

_____

_____

_____

_____

_____

_____

_____

Example: NANCY IS CHIEF OF NURSING in a busy psychiatric hospital. She is thrust into chaos and trauma during the course of her whole day. She also has two young children who want her attention the minute she enters the house at the end of her day.

Nancy keeps three stones handy. She keeps one in her uniform pocket, one at her desk, and one in her car.

When she does 1 Stone at work, she is able to maintain a sense of calm even amidst all the activity.

Using this strategy before she enters her home, Nancy says she gains perspective, and it helps her leave work at work when re-entering her personal life.

She says, "1 Stone helps me be more present for myself and my family, and it helps me handle whatever comes my way."

Affirmation:

Each moment I take to calm myself
I expand my reservoir of peace.

Notes & Insights:

Mere mental rehearsal produces as big a change in the cortex as the physical practice.

Dr. Alvaro Pascual-Leone, Harvard University

living your OASIS

CONGRATULATIONS!

You have completed your *OASIS in the Overwhelm 28 Day Guide* for rewiring your brain from chaos to calm. Hopefully you are seeing positive changes in your natural responses to stress.

Remember the two things we know for sure – stress is here to stay, and habits are hard to change. Yet by now you know that with awareness, tools and practice, you can consciously manage your reactions to overwhelm and carve out new healthy habits.

We designed these past four weeks to jumpstart that journey for you, and you made it through! Now you know that you can create your own OASIS any time, anywhere.

stop and celebrate!

Before anything else, we urge you to take a moment and celebrate your success. Mark this event with a real treat – small or big – whatever you like. Do something as a reminder to what you have already accomplished, and want to continue for your health and happiness. Get a massage. Go out with friends. Take a mental-wellness day. Go to the beach!

Whatever you do, do not skip by too fast here. Do something that lets you relax or play and bask in the glow of a journey well-traveled.

There are so many ways you can keep yourself afloat and flourishing when it comes to managing your stress, while you deepen your new habits. Here are a handful for you:

tap your strengths

REVIEW THE ACKNOWLEDGE YOUR STRENGTHS ASSESSMENT on page 27. The activities, behaviors and tactics that you know already work for you are the ones to tap into whenever the situation calls for them. For example, if you know you are good at asking for help from friends, keep it up . . . if you have some great hobbies that relax you, be sure you are making time for them, even when and *especially* when you are most stressed.

bridge the gaps

YOU WILL GET EVEN FURTHER by diving in to focus on areas that you instinctively know require more attention. You can remind yourself of which areas these are by referring to the self-assessment on pages 29-30. If there were areas that required a deeper look, this is a great place to put some of your time and energy.

make OASIS a ritual

AS YOU KNOW, THE BEST WAY to remember the OASIS Strategies and call them up easily when needed is to practice on a regular basis – just like building a muscle. It is easiest to practice regularly when you tie it to another habit you already have. For example, you can do a 4-D when you first wake; do a 3-B-C right before your morning cup of coffee; keep a stone on your nightstand and do that exercise before turning off the light.

Tagging on your OASIS practice will help make it a ritual without your feeling stressed to "fit in" yet another task. This is meant to lighten your load, not load you up!

tune in often

WHEN YOU ARE FEELING STRESSED and want to figure out which OASIS Strategy to use, you can always tune in and trust your intuition and your body. Take some deep breaths, focus, and then ask these questions:

- In what way am I most drained or stressed right now?
- What needs my attention most right now?
- What would be most useful for me right now?

After hearing your answers, read the choices below that include a corresponding strategy. Decide which of the answers resonates for you this moment. Take your best guess and start here. This is just to give you an idea. You may decide to provide yourself with another answer. There is no right answer. You will know.

- **My body and/or mind are feeling stuck or stiff**. I want a way I can stretch my body or I could use a broader or more creative view.   **4-D** page 33

- **I feel in chaos or turmoil**. I want to stop the whirl and bring my situation from craziness to calm. I could use something that brings me to the now and helps me make conscious choices.   **3-B-C** page 49

- **My typical responses to stress are not working** and I need a better way to deal with things; I want to get to the heart of my habitual responses to stress, and change them to healthier and more productive ones for me.

  Cue-2-Do page 65

- **I am in the mode of doing and not being.** I want something for my times of disconnectedness, when I am on auto-drive or over-drive. I could use something simple, brief and meditative to slow me down to balance my whole self in any moment.   **1 Stone** page 85

share the strategies

ONE OF THE BEST WAYS to solidify a new skill is to teach it to others. This is the best scenario of all. Not only will you give valuable life tools to a friend, co-worker or loved one, you will engrain your new habits as well!

travel in good company

YOU CAN ALWAYS PARTNER WITH A FRIEND as you continue to practice the OASIS Strategies. This will absolutely reinforce your abilities with the techniques. Make some commitments to each other and then check in on each other's progress. Accountability can really make a difference.

Also, make a list of who your own personal support network will be when it comes to your future management of stress. Whenever you are in need of some extra support, friends, family, or even expert coaches like us can really make a difference.

Remember that it is a sign of strength to ask for help when you know you need it, and it validates for others that we're all just human.

give yourself credit!

THIS ONE BEARS REPEATING. Stop periodically to acknowledge how you are making headway – even when you feel you're taking one step forward and two steps back. Since what you focus on will expand, keep putting your attention on what is working for you, and keep moving forward.

We wish you a beautiful life with peace, health and happiness. Enjoy your journey!

Millie, Jill, Ginny

> Allow yourself to trust joy and embrace it.
> You will find you dance with everything.
>
> Ralph Waldo Emerson

Notes & Insights:

YOUR OASIS GUIDES

MILLIE, JILL, AND GINNY each operate their own coaching businesses. They coach individuals and groups, train, speak, facilitate, and conduct retreats.

photo by M.J. Fiedler, *Connecticut Post*

MILLIE GRENOUGH is an Executive Coach, international keynote speaker, and award-winning author who is known for her ability to inspire people to do what they thought was impossible. She has taught non-singers to sing, shy speakers to speak confidently in public, Type A personalities to work smarter, warring parties to work together, and harried CEOs and parents to breathe easier.

Millie is happiest when she has time and space to enjoy life's many facets. She is an avid biker, hiker, meditator, wife, grandmom, and Clinical Instructor in Social Work of Psychiatry at the Yale University School of Medicine.

A graduate of The Coaches Training Institute, Millie is certified by the International Coach Federation, is an EMDR-Level II Therapist, and is one of ten people worldwide named Master Synergist in the body/mind Rubenfeld Synergy Method®.

An international Career and Life Coach, JILL BERQUIST specializes in helping high-performance adrenalizers unplug the treadmill, and plug into themselves for success on their path to greater freedom and fulfillment. Jill's unique blend of the practical, intuitive, and inspirational swiftly gets to the heart of the situation, and is the catalyst to transformational results.

photo by Edward Rudman

Jill lives in beautiful New England with her husband and two spirited young daughters. She unplugs herself through dance, play, tai chi, friends, precious moments alone, and any waterfront.

Jill is a Professional Certified Coach through the International Coach Federation and a founder of the Connecticut Collaborative of Professional Coaches. She is a recognized Life Blueprint™ coach and authorized facilitator of the Now What™ career and life direction program, as well as an Authorized OASIS Trainer.

photo by Brian Ambrose

VIRGINIA KRAVITZ, a sought-after Career and Life Coach, has always been fascinated by how people make meaningful change and create lives that delight them. Ginny founded *In the Current*™ to help accomplished professionals use their restlessness as the door to something bigger and to start living with a greater sense of joy and abandon.

Ginny resides in Scottsdale, Arizona and creates her own OASIS by dancing with the music turned up, reserving quiet time in the morning, practicing yoga, and laughing often with her husband, family, and friends.

A graduate of Coach U, Ginny is also a member of the International Coach Federation. She is a recognized Life Blueprint™ coach and authorized facilitator of the Now What™ career and life direction program, as well as an Authorized OASIS Trainer.

TO INQUIRE ABOUT COACHING or to invite us to present to your organization, please reach us at:

- Millie Grenough
  millie@grenough.com
  www.grenough.com

- Jill Berquist
  jill@berquistcoaching.com
  www.berquistcoaching.com

- Virginia Kravitz
  ginny@inthecurrent.com
  www.inthecurrent.com

FOR MORE INFORMATION concerning OASIS products or programs, to order the OASIS Guide as a book or e-book, and for a complete list of Authorized OASIS Trainers:

- www.oasisintheoverwhelm.com
- orders@oasisintheoverwhelm.com
- 1-203-888-4733

WE WELCOME YOUR FEEDBACK about this Guide. Please let us know about your successes, your challenges, and your own ideas about using OASIS in your life. To share your ideas and stories, send an email to:

- story@oasisintheoverwhelm.com